Remedy

Remedy

Emily Bridget Taylor

Bijou Press

Remedy

First published in Australia in 2024
by Bijou Press
bijou-press.com

All Rights Reserved.

Poetry by Emily Bridget Taylor
www.emilybridgettaylor.com
@emilybridgettaylor

Thank you for complying with the copyright laws by not reproducing, scanning, or distributing any part of it in any form without permission, except for the purpose of review and promotion of the work.

Interior and Cover design by Rebecca Rijsdijk
rebeccarijsdijk.com

Thanks for reading.

Trigger Warning

This poetry book contains content that may be emotionally distressing or triggering for certain readers. Some poems explore sensitive topics including but not limited to trauma, mental health, violence, and loss. Read with care, and never be afraid to ask for help.

Dedication

For those who refuse to be swallowed. Who climb
back up the throat that claimed them, to fall from the
mouth as sacred words in the

                      dazzling

                                open

                                            air

                                                        that calls their name.

Contents

The Falling ……………………..……..page 11

The Severing ………………..…………page 27

The Healing ……………..……………page 71

The Resurrecting ……………................…page 93

The Falling

Spill

Ink is the blood of my craft, and I'll spill it all when it comes to *you*.

Remedy

The Constellation of You

They were the days
the summer baked
freckles into your neck
and I kissed every one.

No one knew where we were
in the open air
of our youth,
but I knew –

I was sunlight-drunk
and lost
in the constellation of you.

Midnight Bus

On the midnight bus
we ride
your hand holds mine
the other
clasps a paperback novel.

Imagine –
the black outside
is a silent sea
and you and me
swim endlessly
in the silver light
of a perishing moon.

Remedy

You are Golden

Golden slumber, autumn-time
leather tassel, vintage find
fragile needle
of the pine –
glint in the emerald of your eye.

Forgetting Plans

Play me that psychedelic rhythm – let's forget our plans,
for a minute. Drink our honey tea, bask in the sunroom.
I don't care about the weather or nice friends or *tidiness*.
Go ahead and play me that song, the one that we like –
the one that makes us move.

Remedy

Wolves

It was a kind of madness
the way you loved me –
deep
in the throat
of our youth.

We were a howl flung
to the mouth of the
darkness,
a monologue whispered
to the face of the moon.

Adoration

You wore me down, with your love.
Like a river to a stone,
your adoration to my heart.

Remedy

Second Coming

You looked at my body like it was
the Second Coming.
Lay your hands on me, I said – salvation is here.

EMILY BRIDGET TAYLOR

All Seasons Love

Find someone

who sees in you

the light of stars and moons

and loves you,

whether you burn

or fade,

shine

or shy away –

an all-seasons love

in sunshine and rain.

Remedy

Green Eyes

When the moon

swallows me up

and I feel like

even the stars can't save me now –

your green eyes sing me home.

Bridges

I have come to learn –
love is fully seeing someone and accepting them
choosing them, regardless.

No matter who you look at
if you look long enough
you're going to see flaws –
and they will see yours.

Sometimes the flaws are gut-wrenching –
      3 am tears, screams of why, despair in the dark.

But in the light, the answers come
and that bridge – between your heart and theirs
strengthens –
because you chose them
in the dark.

Remedy

Remedy

If my love craves blood
I will give it to him.
Grow talons from my fingertips and rip
at the body, and the skin,
of whatever pleases him.

If my love craves worship
I will give it to him.
Draw veins of gold
from the rose-crush within,
crown his head with flowers and sing
a song of adoration.

If my love craves remedy
I will give it to him.
Gather herbs and ivy,
lay them by his sleeping side
and watch the dark unfold to dawn
with healing in its wings.

The Severing

I'm Losing You

Sometimes the days seem long. I light a candle I can't afford – you play a song to change the mood, bring the beat back. You seem a million miles away. I have learned that loneliness hangs from my lips since they kissed yours.

Remedy

I'd Do it All Again

All they see
are all the things
I do for you.

But I see
green eyes and laughter
on a Monday afternoon,
blackness and thunder
the absence of your father
and scars that can't be hidden
by painted skin alone.

So, a few more coffees
a Netflix show,
and I'll be okay.

My therapist said
we are healing together
and I believe in that –
I believe
in the long road home
I believe
it won't be too long
I believe
we'll be home soon.

Remedy

Dance Again

When will you come to me?
I want you to touch me, again
I want you to rip my shirt open
For my neck
to fall back
in your hands,
for my ribcage to shiver with the force
of being reborn.

> I have grown quiet, like the dark of night
>   in the folds of the lily.
> I have fallen still, like the frozen winter lake.
> I am a hollow sepulchre, carved in white marble.

EMILY BRIDGET TAYLOR

I need to dance, again
    to be decanted
like fine wine
    all over your fine plans –

It is not in my nature
    to be so young
    and so unmoved –
    move me.

Remedy

Voyeur

Your movements, child-like, have grown
> desperate in the dark.
Pills fall across the table
> like pieces of shattered glass.
I wonder how long this can last
> when every day wanders
further from the past
> in which I knew you.

What great veil
> must I remove
to catch the memory
> of your youth,
or hear the music
> of your laugh?

EMILY BRIDGET TAYLOR

It slips through my hands
like water,
from lover to voyeur –
I pray to swim
in your tides again.

Remedy

It Kills Me

I kept giving
pieces of myself
to you
as small gifts

wrapped in golden paper
that you just assembled
on your shelf
as ornaments.

All this time
what I wanted
what I longed for –
was for you to unwrap me.

Stagger

Your nails, overgrown
my hair, a nest of knots
I am Rochester

pacing the moors, and you
my phantom, my wraith
my cackling secret

reach through walls
to clutch at my heart
with fingers stained in blood.

How has this stagger
in the dark
come to be called *love*?

Remedy

Tapestry

I called him a *professional victim*
he slammed the door
called me a whore
and now there is a fire
he has lit to keep me warm.

I remember
not that word, but the feeling
and I wonder if I can ever escape him –
the first victim
whose persecutor was also a woman

because patterns repeat in me
hooks, calls
weave into my skin
a tapestry of shadows
after *years* of stitching

EMILY BRIDGET TAYLOR

and I wonder if
soon I'll be
hanging from
the
w
a
l
l

Remedy

Paranoia

You make a ministry of misery,
        bleeding sorrow all over me.
You serve the bread of preservation
           in your Temple of Paranoia.

Take it like the sacrament, you say.

But I don't want to –
it makes me weary
I spit it up.

Eat, eat. They will kill you in your sleep.

I am the last of your disciples
looking out the window
where the enemy is to charge.

I feel like my heart
could weep
until it was empty
seeing you this way, again.

A solitary priest –
chasing demons from your dreams.

The water of suffering
>	runs heavy
in our blood,
>	poured out in a cup
next to the bread.

You hand it to me,
I push it aside.

Drink, drink. This is our final stand.

I want to say
so many things to you –
you have abandoned reason
in the name of freedom
but
I
see
chains
like vipers behind you.

Remedy

Dead Loop

Our apologies
        circle round each other
like two snakes
        hissing tunes
                melancholy.

        We shed tears
like scales
        wishing it could be fixed
that we could be
        in love again.

You whisper –
    sorry
        for being
                who I told you I was,
                      all along, all along, all along.

Why can't I do the thing?

The time makes
dumb mockery
of me

I am thick with sleep
an hour too late
embezzling

my potential –
it is a curse, to be filled with life
and hesitation.

Remedy

The Dystopia of Us

In the dystopia of us,
        a cavity grows –
deep, wide, and cold, within me.
The miner is grief,
and gold there is none –
and all the eyes, of everyone,
        bear down like blackened suns.

The cavity is
        a shadow mouth
        a dormant spring
like a garden dead, it withered lies,
in the hollows of my eyes.
Now I see your strange demise
        through a hanging veil or falling rain,
distorting us within the frame.

EMILY BRIDGET TAYLOR

I wear the ghost of you
        on my lips, in my lungs.
I kiss the air and breathe the dust,
           making love to the mirage
of a distant memory steeped in rust,
and fruitless days that have passed –

        to a nothingness, at last.

Remedy

Haunting

I have become a hunted thing.
Haunted by caring ghosts
that come for me.

My nails grow long and thin
they alarm. And my hair
trails behind me, a lonely river.

They shut the door, so no one sees.
I do not show my face to the sun
or the moon – though she understands

what it is
to be a beastly thing – an incantation
that shrinks, shape-shifts, sans heartbeat.

EMILY BRIDGET TAYLOR

I am not their sunshine girl, anymore –
my smile is the edge of a hacksaw
my fingers, curiosities
that sniff and see
and feel
along the skin of reason.

Remedy

Drowning

I held you by the hand
just above the water line
white knuckle
sinew buckle
I held you

In white
rushing
water
I never wondered
if you would
pull
me
in
with you –
but you did.

I Will Wear Your Shadow

Through the valley. Through the moors. Wherever I might find a trace of you on the wind, I wander. But you left nothing. I wish you had – I would have worn the shadow of you *all day* if I could have.

Remedy

Separation – A Memoir

For the last two weeks
I have brushed my hair
with a yellow plastic comb
brought home in a biohazard bag
courtesy of the asylum
because my youngest brother
who spoke to me on the phone
while smoking a cigarette
listening to *The Iliad*
keeps forgetting to return
the hairbrush I left behind in his bathroom
the night the moon was new
and I left you

EMILY BRIDGET TAYLOR

In this way
because of him (and really, you)
even in my hair
you make your presence known
while you're in an apartment
somewhere, getting stoned
I am here *untangling*

I wish you would leave me alone.

Remedy

Devotion

I loved you
as a bright green jewel
the stories of the sea
tattooed to your skin
the fire of stars
in the atlas of your eyes.

I loved you
in the heartache of ambition
when you longed
to be transfigured
into the star you bled to be –
you were already famous, to me.

EMILY BRIDGET TAYLOR

I loved you
in the temple
when angels cried
between the arches
of our surrender,
hands bound in priestly stole.

I loved you
     in the cradle
  of the mentally
        unstable
when horses galloped through the walls
        on an afternoon in May –
and you were convinced
        that it was night
           when it was day.

I loved you
when the crowds came
and when they didn't.

Remedy

When the world laughed,
or sneered.
When you became
a child in sleep
or shivered
as you lit
a fire in the keep
and lost
the
words
to
speak –

How can you abandon me?

Still Breathing

Your mouth became the *tomb* I crawled out of.

Remedy

Undeserving

They called me by your name – is there a higher form of love?

Vampire

I have worn black
the entire month of June
to a funeral no one can see
and the deceased
fantasy of you
is the body on which I feast.

Remedy

Impaled

These days my heart
is a jagged stone.
It doesn't beat, it doesn't
break.
It presses cold
against skin and moan,
blood and feeling –
it is a tomb without memorial
a captive bird without song
cinder fire, come and gone.

EMILY BRIDGET TAYLOR

Small Mercies

The best thing you left was Temazepam – at least then
I could sleep with no thought of you.

Remedy

Unchosen

All those boys
who said
they loved me

fade to ash
in my hands
as I stand

on the threshold
of this damned
wasteland.

My shoulders sag,
made of letters
sent in heat

EMILY BRIDGET TAYLOR

now grey and curling

fluttering on the wings

of yearning – unfulfilled.

In galleries, they ask

who is the girl

on the moors

the one in the painting

lamenting her wanderings?

self-portrait

Remedy

Creature

My mother would not
recognise me
I have grown beastly in hibernation

The one who was my protector
went away with the winter
and when I look in the mirror
yellow eyes blink back at me.

I have made a den
of bones, my wet nose
maps

EMILY BRIDGET TAYLOR

the nooks

the edges

I tear holes in my clothes

the skin of my neck

chilled with sweat

thickens

I alone defend my door –

a mouth that leads

to the earth

to my claws.

Remedy

Hidden

The cold was a friend clung to in my loneliest hour. Soon it will be taken by the glare of Summer – her expectations, her white noise. They dance, but all I want is to run – where all within can be hidden. Dissolve like snow on the tongue of the river. Fade as mist in the shadows, silver. My treasured season – rain forever.

Leave Me Alone

Texting someone *I still love you* without consent is a form of emotional abuse.

Remedy

You're Not Invited

Let me
let you go.
I need to attend
the funeral of us
to make sense
of it all.
I need time
to smoke our moments
in a cigarette salute
and watch as ash falls
and every feeling of you
slips through my fingers
to the sky
as fumes.

Running

There was no moon the night I made my escape. The onyx sky enveloped me. Your last words, a vapour – dispelled to the mouthless stars. *Let them have them* I said –

the witch has been released.

Remedy

Mad House

And she found that the madness
was not a death knell –
it was her liberation.
Welcome to The Mad House.

The Healing

Strange Disappearance

God help the next man who breaks my heart.

Remedy

Hive

Could have been the honey.
Could have been the bee.
Could have been the *goddamn hive* –
if only you'd let me be.

EMILY BRIDGET TAYLOR

Unpartnered

I try to be everything I need, but I'm so tired of being alone.

Remedy

I Shouldn't Be Having These Thoughts

I look at you
and wonder if
you are a taxi
I can hop into
for a while

Do you have someone at home?
Are they around?
Would they care,
if you drove me through town?

Who would it hurt?
I'd fade in the sun
like blue jeans
like the American Dream
like it never even happened

EMILY BRIDGET TAYLOR

Life is a series of moments
this would be just one –
let me in.

Remedy

Anxious Attachment

For some
I love you
is enough.

But for me to feel loved
the sun must be
lassoed from the sky
cast on a golden string
and fastened to my neck
by the hunter's hand.

I must be looked at
like I am
a sea they can never reach
the bottom of –
but even then
I won't believe it.

EMILY BRIDGET TAYLOR

Can I be yours?

You called me baby, once.
I caught the word
in the middle of a sentence
in the middle of you
removing my shirt
I lived on that word
for weeks –
and you never knew.

Remedy

Begging For It

You, my most delicious form of self-harm.
Wound me again.

Early Days

I am scared
the more I show
all the ways I hurt,
the less you will love me –
and what I need
more than anything
is the adoration lies buy me.

Remedy

What Did You Expect?

A fool's errand
wrapped in nostalgic perfume –
I really did a number on you.

Metamorphosis

I shed him like a skin and found myself within.

Remedy

Deity

Since he's been gone, I have anointed myself with perfume from the South of France. I have lit candles for myself, created shrines. Picked flowers, too. I have risen with the sun and slept with the moon. I have grown my hair long, like golden sand dunes. And at night, I lie like a star someone, somewhere is wishing on.

Gentle

I have to be
so gentle
with myself these days

gentle
as lilac,
lavender
or the moon on water

gentle,
delicately cradle
my heart
like something soft
and newly born.

Remedy

Seasons

My one goal is to be kind to myself. This is not the season to move mountains – it is the season to bind wounds. To be brave enough to let go of being productive. To let my heart repair and mend. The mountains will still be there, in the end – it is enough to find the courage to begin again.

EMILY BRIDGET TAYLOR

Pack a Silk Eye Mask

Self-love is a long-haul flight.

Remedy

Anointing

She is made of hoaxes. Shadows. Threadbare hope. She gropes in the dark, somewhere between the problem and the solution. Only the white-hot eye of God can see her, but it grows smaller with each phase of the moon. This is the making of her, in the dying of her. The moment a crown of diamonds becomes a crown of thorns. This is the anointing of her, in the falling – rising up to be reborn.

Nectar

Tonight, I feel like a woman –
wrapped in black gossamer silk
flowing like water
down my bare skin.

They say there is a moment
you know you're a woman
and I think
in the moonlight,
seeping through the windowpane
caressing the white melon
of my breast, I know it precisely.

God, I'm a woman –

I'm a woman tonight.

Remedy

Mesmerising

In the twist of your hair and the movement of your hips, I see softness and fight. Volcanic eruption and alpine snow. You are everything that has ever been told – you are everything there is to know.

Siren

You can find her in a turquoise lagoon. Somewhere between a dream and a nightmare. She's the sparkle on the water in the afternoon – and the scales of her send you slithering to her door. To some, she is known as The Siren. To foes, an ocean witch.

To the sailor, the deathless deathless deep.

The Resurrecting

Cradles

Little did I know
the grave I lay down in
was the cradle of your hands –
you were
rebirthing me
all along.

Remedy

Grace

A maple leaf

like a flower

between your teeth

hangs with the last fruit

of summer

waiting for the snap of fall

to become one with the soil.

EMILY BRIDGET TAYLOR

Bleeding brown into brown
its worth is revealed
in the falling, dying, subsuming –
moulded by the hands of Earth
to raise again its face
through the darkness
to the sun
blooming, transcendent grace.

Remedy

Love Divine

I can't believe I wasted time loving someone, something that wasn't You. Who else can boast of a love that understands the language of sighs? That moves mountains for me? That reads my pain, in the palms of my hands and grows roses from them?

There is

    no

        other

           love

                I want to lose a second for.

Formation

There is beauty in
the candle at half-melt,
standing tall in strange
formation
eaten by the flame
but not yet entirely
diminished.

How beautiful we are
when burned,
consumed
on fire,
but not
extinguished.

Remedy

Eye of Heaven

Violent winds slap the face
of The Swan.
Gulls fly in gentle collection –
I feel I could take flight, too.

Far over on Narrows Bridge
cars speck and glitter crawl
and the afternoon haze
obscures Mt Eliza in shadow

and always, the assailing wind
vaults my soul
toward the eye of heaven.

EMILY BRIDGET TAYLOR

Let's Get Lost

If the answers were mountains, I'd know them all.

Remedy

Here

The last light of day
blooms grey,
softly resting like a dove
on my left shoulder.
The olive trees stand silent watch,
tolerating the scratch of my pen,
and the rosemary of remembrance
grows around this veranda,
where at 2 o'clock today
Grandma shared her stories,
about her father and the
installation of lights in the city
and how they denied him entry
three times to the War.

EMILY BRIDGET TAYLOR

In the twilight
the magic
that lies in the dying of the day,
offers its goodbyes in the form
of rain
falling on the tin roof.
Inside, now, Grandma knits –
frogs begin their chorus,
and I remember the time
I felt most safe – was here,
as a child,
and still is here –
at the house in the valley
by the ocean.

Remedy

Ancestors

You were carried here
by so many hands
the hands of your ancestors
pouring your life, like precious water
from cup to cup
passing it forward –
and however unsteady
their hands were
here you are

so live your life
like you are
thousands of years in the making.

Held

Here's to being the mountain –
holding it all
yet being held
by the greatness of Earth
beneath.
Wherever I am –
there you are.

Remedy

A Love Letter to Friendship

Nothing steadies the soul
like someone who knows
your history, and will be
the first to help you write
the next chapter

Someone who loves you
but also loves to evolve –
someone who knows you
but also knows
your higher self.

Sisterhood

When we talk, it's two wind chimes singing. Our notes, high and sweet, echo each other – every cadence, a complimentary colour. If our song were to end, I would never speak again.

Remedy

Manifest

Maybe if we started seeing
ourselves
not as ourselves
but as a friend
someone to look out for
and believe in –
magical things would happen.

It's All Within

Be brave. You will see the sun again. You will hear the songs of stars ricochet from the movements of your hands. Once again, you will breathe *galaxies* into being.

Remedy

Truly Free

I want to be truly free –
to grasp the axis of the sun
hold it like a plaything
afraid of nothing.

Because all those things
that were meant to scare me
bloom like a canopy
of wildflowers holding me.

The more I see
the less I believe
that dangers lurk beneath my feet.

The more I touch
the more I know
fear blossoms where
you let it grow.

Resurrection

Like the smoke, from the flame extinguished –
so too will I rise.

Remedy

Daylight

I will write
our story
in golden, molten ink
my love –
I will write
every dream
every happiness
we ever dreamt of.

I will write
until we take flight
and every doubt
and fear
is lost
in the wash of daylight.

EMILY BRIDGET TAYLOR

To the Women Who Write

If you had never written a word
I would have nothing to say.

I wouldn't have the power to imagine,
to pick up the pen, to name my work.

If you had stopped,
my heart would have deadened
before it even knew to beat –
you carried me without even knowing it.

Tonight, as my candle burns
and my hands tap a writer's dance
I have you to thank –
the named and unnamed
female authors
carrying the future on your shoulders.

Remedy

Ariel

Peel back my skin and you will find –
the art of resurrection.

Gravity

I found mercy
in the shape of your arms.
They say I moved on too fast –
but I don't control
what gravity does.

Remedy

All I Needed

You called in the middle
of the dark blue night
and now I must write
poetry
when I think of you.

Nothing else will do.

All your days
from now until
your purest flight,
will be documented
by my words

I promise you.

EMILY BRIDGET TAYLOR

I may never be
acclaimed,
but it doesn't matter
if one day, the work
distils your essence perfectly

if my lines set you ticking
like a fat gold watch
wound forever –
I will have done
all I ever needed to

all I ever dreamed of.

Remedy

Postcode

They tell you in books that heaven is up a ladder somewhere, among the stars. That if you're lucky, you might see it one day – if you're good enough. But I found it. It lives in the place that finds its postcode

    when you look at me

             and kiss

                      my lips.

EMILY BRIDGET TAYLOR

Long Distance Love

Three moons – then you.
Here I am, again
measuring time
as the distance between
my heart and your hands.

Remedy

Electric

When we are together

        it feels as if we are

the first man and woman

                on Earth.

Cinema

I wrap myself in your words, long after you leave – and the hands of sleep weave your picture between my eyelids. As stars gather, my favourite cinema begins.

Remedy

Hanging On

i –

It has begun
to feel
like
forget days
months
even the moon
and her cycles –

I am measuring time
by how long
it is
until I see
you again –
I only
have
to
hang
on
that long.

ii –

On the other side
of these listless hours
is a steady breathing
a chest to lie against
that rises
and falls
like the ocean
always reaching out for me.

It's you I see –
on the other side
of these listless hours.

Remedy

iii –

You are worth
holding on to.
For you – I disown limit.
For you – I hold
the hands of distance.

In the lullaby of night
the threat of loneliness looms,
but this I will bless
with a reverent kiss –

the moonlight on my lips, only you.

Rainbows

Have there been others? Of course, there have been others. Look at you. Look at me. We know the pull of beauty. The way hands reach for love and long to show it. But what does it matter? I reach for you, only you. You reach for me. All the others fade. They were mist before the rain *really* started falling. And now I'm drenched in you. Let's kiss in this rain, and make love to the moment of us. Why would we cry at the mist of distant mornings when the sun is in

full

iridescent

bloom?

Let's make rainbows of our downpour.

Remedy

Promise

When my time comes, your memory will slip with me through the stars and far past the melting moon. *I will never stop* thinking about you.

EMILY BRIDGET TAYLOR

Infinity

Count the shells as they cluster
on the tide of the full moon

Number the shades of yellow
in the crescendo of afternoon

Account for the shape of water
as waves unspool

Try as you might you could never
measure all the ways I love you.

Remedy

Never Let Me Go

Lord have mercy
on your soul
if I have to write
break up poetry
about you.

I'd write it in my own blood.
I'd write until
there was nothing
left of me
in the annihilation of us.

Perpetuity

Your beauty is deathless in
my ink –
the wine of immortality

Letter to the Reader

You have arrived at the end. Now do it – do the thing. The thing that flutters in your heart like a moth longing to be *released* –

let it out

let it out

let it out.

Do whatever it takes to be free – *you were born for this.*

Leave a Review

About the Author

Emily Bridget Taylor is a poet, artist and performer. Her words and imagery are inspired by honey-filled days of light and love, and the dark hours between – the duality that is Life's gift. In 2021, Emily began sharing her poetry online. What followed was a surprising, magical journey in which her words and images resonated around the world, connecting especially with women. Her poetry collection *Remedy*, art series *Remedy for Walls* and performance poetry touch on themes of love, trauma, self-care and healing. Her artistic calling is to dissolve shame in all its forms. Follow her journey at www.emilybridgettaylor.com and @emilybridgettaylor on socials.

About the Book

Remedy is a collection of poetry for those who refuse to be extinguished. It is a story told in four parts, each part mending a different kind of pain. Remedy will take you by the hand through the falling, severing, healing and resurrecting – giving you the courage to begin again.

"Remedy is a powerful collection that channels strength, love and hope. The poems within this volume remind us what it is to be human and vulnerable. They highlight that we are emphatically bigger than the moments we experience, and that our strength arises out of knowing who we are, where we have come from, and from trusting that one of the greatest loves of all is the love we have for ourselves" - *Maria Papas, author of Skimming Stones*

"Emily Bridget Taylor has crafted a collection of poems that spark and fall apart as they explore love, break-ups, the gothic noir and mist-covered moors. Here, love is presented as luminous, messy, gut wrenching and as devastatingly beautiful. At all times there is a tinge of darkness while, in the short prose poems, Taylor's voice soars to new heights. Remedy is soul-food, scars and all" - *Scott-Patrick Mitchell, author of Clean*

"To engage in the pursuit of delight is a meaningful way to pass the time. To lament, however, is something many don't understand the power of. Prophetic poet Emily holds hands with the power of both, to lead her readers into a pathway of self-discovery. This book will be a balm to a post-pandemic world" - *Amanda Viviers, author, Executive Director of Compassion Australia*

www.ingramcontent.com/pod-product-compliance
Lightning Source LLC
Chambersburg PA
CBHW022018290426
44109CB00015B/1220